Contents

KU-612-464

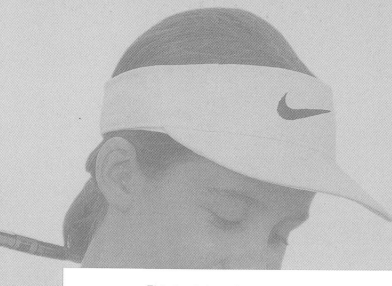

Golf

Bernie Blackall

Heinemann LIBRARY

First published in Great Britain by Heinemann Library,
Halley Court, Jordan Hill, Oxford OX28EJ,
a division of Reed Educational & Professional Publishing Ltd.

01 00 99 98 97
10 9 8 7 6 5 4 3 2 1

Original design by Karen Young
Edited by Angelique Campbell-Muir
Illustrated by Vasja Koman
Paged by Patricia Tsiatsias
Photography by Malcolm Cross
Production by Alexandra Tannock
Printed in Hong Kong by Wing King Tong

ISBN 0431 08503 X

British Library
Cataloguing in Publication data:

Blackall, Bernie.
    Golf. - (Top Sport)
    1. Golf – Juvenile literature.
    I. Title
    796.3'52

This title is also available in hardback edition ISBN 0431 08498 X.

Acknowledgements

The publisher would like to thank the following for their kind assistance:
Rebel Sport, Prahran
Students from Armadale Primary School – Robert Klein, Nicola Murdock,
Khoa Nguyen, Mimosa Rizzo, Andrew Scott, Charlotte Sheck-Shaw,
Zheng Yu.

Photographs supplied by:
Tony Marshall / Empics, page 6
John Marsh / Empics, page 7
The Bridgeman Art Library: 15th Century golfers, page 8

Special thanks to Margaret Berriman, and Geoffrey Fink, Australian PGA,
for their assistance during the production of this book.
Every attempt has been made to trace and acknowledge copyright.
Where the attempt has been unsuccessful, the publishers would be pleased
to hear from the copyright owner so any omission or error can be rectified.

About golf

Golf is a game played on an outdoor course. The aim of golf is to hit a small ball into a series of holes using a club, taking as few **strokes** as possible to do so.

A golf course is usually made up of 18 **holes**. A hole refers to the whole playing area between the teeing off area and the putting green where the actual hole is located. Each of the holes is made up of three distinct sections:

- the tee
- the fairway
- the green.

The golfer's first shot, the **tee shot**, is hit from the **tee** – a flat, well mown area about 5 metres square. To make it easier to hit, the ball may be placed on a small plastic or wooden tee. The tee is pushed into the ground and the ball sits on top of the tee, off the grass. This is the only time the ball can be placed on a tee.

After driving from the tee the golfer aims to land the ball on the **fairway**. The fairway is the stretch of ground that runs from the tee to the green. The grass on the fairway is cut short. If the ball lands in the rough – on either side of the fairway – it is more difficult to hit because the grass is longer.

There are other areas on the fairway that golfers try to avoid, such as **bunkers** and **water hazards**. Bunkers are depressions

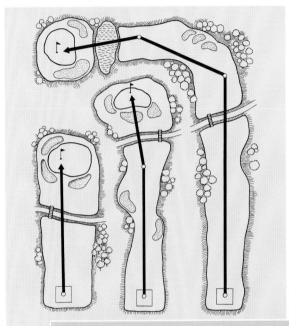

This is what typical par 3, par 4 and par 5 holes might look like on a golf course.

filled with sand. Water hazards can include lakes, ponds, streams and ditches. All of these **hazards** complicate the golfer's progress to the **green**.

The green is the third part of the hole, and is where the actual hole is located. The grass on the green is carefully prepared and very smooth so that the ball can run along the ground to the hole. The hole is 10.8 centimetres in diameter and is sunk into the ground.

The **flagstick**, a removable pole about 2 metres tall with a flag on top, sits in the hole. This gives golfers an aiming point when they are too far away to see the actual hole.

Golf highlights

For most people golf is a skilful and enjoyable game that offers fresh air, exercise, companionship and an element of competition. However, for many years golf has been a highly paid professional sport whose leaders are known world wide.

Jack Nicklaus - the greatest golfer

Jack Nicklaus is the greatest golfer of modern times. He was born in Ohio, USA in 1940 and by the age of 19 had won the American Amateur Championship. He turned professional in 1961 and in 1962 won his first US Open Championship, beating the great Arnold Palmer in a play-off.

Initially, Jack was not very popular, probably because he was beating former heroes like Palmer and Gary Player. However, people began to appreciate his golfing skills. His very success made the game exciting and drew people to the game who had never thought of playing.

Jack won 20 Major Championships altogether and had more than 70 Tour victories. He now leads the Seniors' Tour.

The Tiger Woods phenomenon

Tiger Woods is the next Jack Nicklaus. His golfing achievements have attracted a new audience to golf. He has become a role model for black people in Europe as well as the US.

Tiger Woods hits a golf ball higher, straighter and further (269 metres) than any other golfer.

Tiger Woods, who started to play golf almost before he could walk.

At 15 he became the youngest winner of the US Junior Amateur Championship. In 1994, at the age of 18, he was the US Amateur Champion and successfully defended the title in 1995 and 1996. He turned professional later in 1996.

He broke all records when he won The Masters at Augusta in 1997:
- youngest winner of The Masters
- largest winning margin
- lowest final round score.

And Tiger Woods is set to break yet more records, this time financial. In 6 months he won more than $12 million. He has a 5-year, $60 million sponsorship deal with Nike and a $1 million deal with Titleist, the equipment manufacturer.

Nick Faldo

Nick Faldo is one of the best-known European players. He was the first to win the PGA Tour's Player of the Year in 1990 and led the rankings for 81 consecutive weeks.

Faldo took up golf at the age of 14 and soon became a champion amateur and later turned professional. Perhaps Faldo is best known for rebuilding his swing. With his new swing he went on to win three Open Championships and three Masters titles. He has been a regular member of the Ryder Cup team. (The Ryder Cup is a team competition played between US and European golf professionals.)

Laura Davies - the longest hitter

England is also home to one of the leading players on the women's professional tour. She has won both British and American Open titles and in 1996 became leading money winner on both European and US Tours. Laura has led the way for many women golfers showing that women can play golf as well

Laura Davies hits the ball further than many men professionals.

as men, can attract both spectators and sponsors to golf courses and can make a name for themselves playing golf.

St Andrews - the home of golf

Scotland is where you will find St Andrews, home to the most famous golf course in the world.

The linksland (the ground between, or linking, the sea and the farmland) was given to the people of the town in medieval times. They used it for rabbiting and cutting turf and, increasingly, as somewhere to play sport – archery, football and golf. Golf became more and more popular until it was the only game that was played. In 1754 the Society of St Andrews Golfers was formed and in 1834 it received a royal accolade and became the Royal and Ancient Golf Club of St Andrews, known universally as The R and A.

History

The earliest forms of club and ball games were played in Ancient Rome, Medieval France and the Netherlands.

The Romans used a bent stick and a leather ball stuffed with feathers to play a game which was like golf. 'Paganica', as the game was called, expanded from the Roman Empire throughout Europe.

A game called 'kolven' was played in Holland. Players used a ball and stick to hit two stumps at each end of a court. The ball was bigger and heavier than the golf ball used today. The word 'golf' probably derived from the Dutch word 'kolf'.

While these ancient forms of club and ball games were similar in nature to golf, there is widespread agreement that the modern game began in Scotland in the 16th Century. The ancient story tells of a bored shepherd who was hitting stones with a crook (crooked stick). When one of these stones landed in a rabbit burrow, a fellow shepherd challenged him to a competition. They tried to hit a 'hole in one' by hitting small stones towards the rabbit hole.

The game of golf that we know today has developed from a combination of these early games. From these beginnings golf has grown to become a truly international pastime, enjoyed by millions of people all over the world.

An illustration of 15th Century Flemish golfers.

What you need to play

Golf can be a very expensive game but need not be for the beginner. Keen golfers can spend considerable amounts of money on a range of clubs to help improve their score. But, as a beginner, a basic kit to get you started will consist of:

- a number of golf balls
- 3-wood
- 3, 5 and 7 irons
- a wedge iron
- a putter
- a golf bag.

All these items can be bought second-hand.

The ball

The golf ball is made of rubber with a hard plastic outer cover and has a diameter of 4.27cm. The surface is dimpled which helps it to fly more efficiently through the air.

The ball can be any colour, although the traditional colour is white. On a frosty morning you will need to use a coloured ball.

A golf bag is designed to carry all the equipment a golfer needs. Most golfers carry a rain suit and an extra sweater. In summer they may need sun protection.

What you need to play

Clubs

There are three basic types of golf clubs:
- woods – numbered 1 to 7
- irons – numbered 1 to 10 (including wedges)
- putters.

Except for the putter, each club has only one striking face which usually has grooves on it. The face, on one side of the head, is the part of the club that makes contact with the ball.

This is an example of the 14 clubs a golfer can choose to carry. From left to right, these are: 1, 3, 4 and 5 woods; 3, 4, 5, 6, 7, 8 and 9 irons; pitching wedge; sand iron; putter.

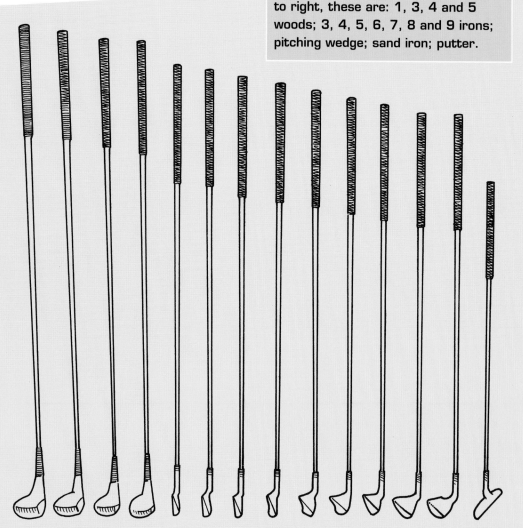

The length of the shaft (the long part of the club from the head to the handle) and angle of the face vary from club to club. Steeply angled (or lofted) faces lift the ball higher but don't send it as far.

The **wood** has a head of wood, light metal or carbon. The usual woods are numbered 1 to 5 and are used for long shots or drives. Woods hit the ball the furthest. The longest hitting club is the number 1 wood (or driver).

Irons are numbered from 1 to 10. The lower the number of the club the greater the distance the ball will travel. The head of the iron is usually metal and the shaft is shorter than that of the wood.

The sand **wedge** has a very short face and flat sole. It is used to get under the ball and hit it up. Golfers use a wedge to slide through the sand when the ball lands in a bunker. The wedge is the shortest hitting iron as it sends the ball virtually straight up into the air.

A **putter** is a metal club used to play the ball on the putting green. Putters come in many different shapes.

Other equipment

Golfers need a golf bag to carry their clubs, balls and other equipment. A trolley might also be useful to wheel around the heavy bag.

In order to improve their grip most golfers wear a glove. Right handed golfers wear one on their left hand; left-handed golfers on their right.

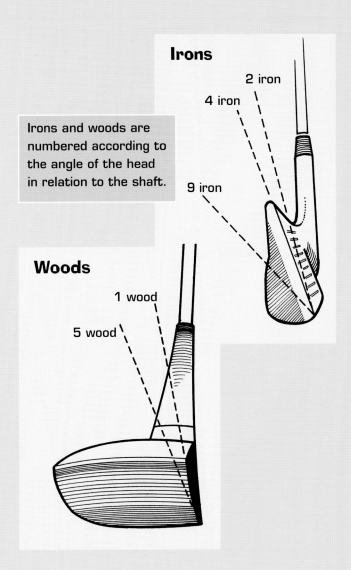

Irons

2 iron

4 iron

9 iron

Irons and woods are numbered according to the angle of the head in relation to the shaft.

Woods

1 wood

5 wood

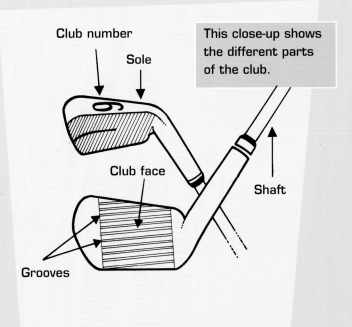

Club number

Sole

Club face

Shaft

Grooves

This close-up shows the different parts of the club.

Rules

Scoring

The purpose of golf is to hit the ball into the hole and to record as few strokes as possible in doing so. Each time the ball is hit the player registers one stroke.

Each hole on the course is given a rating depending on its length. Termed **par**, this figure is determined by the distance from the tee to the hole, and the difficulty of the terrain.

For example, a short hole – about 120–150 metres – would be par 3. A skilful golfer should sink the ball in 3 shots or fewer on a par 3 hole. A distance of 271 metres would be a par 4. A player who took 4 shots to hit the ball into this hole would have scored par.

The par of a particular course is used to measure a player's performance. A golfer's **handicap** is calculated from the par for the course and the golfer's average score. A golfer with an average score of 98 on a par 72 course would have a handicap of 26, because the average score is 26 shots more than par. A very good golfer who completes a round in an average of 72 strokes would have a handicap of 0 (called scratch). Handicapping allows golfers of all standards to compete equally against one another.

Clubs

A golfer can carry a maximum of 14 clubs. It is up to the individual golfer which clubs are used to make up that total.

Playing the ball

The ball must be played from where it lands. Generally, if your ball has lodged in an awkward position you are not allowed to move it. You are permitted to repair damage to the green caused by ball marks. Loose stones, leaves or twigs can be removed but the ball must not be moved. If this happens on the fairway and the ball is moved the golfer suffers a penalty of one stroke which is added to the score.

Teeing off

Each player's ball is hit from the first teeing ground. The ball may be placed on the ground or on a wooden or plastic tee. The next shot is played by the golfer whose ball is furthest from the pin. There-after, the player who has the lowest score on a previous hole drives first. This player is said to have the **honour**.

When hitting from the tee area, the ball may be placed on a tee so that it is easier to hit. This is the only place on the golf course where a tee can be used.

Lost or out of bounds

If your ball is lost or lands on ground that is **out of bounds**, you play another shot from as near as possible to the spot from where the original shot was played. A one shot penalty is added to your score and you must also count the shot that lost the ball or put it out of bounds. Different rules apply if your ball lands in a water hazard.

Hazards

When your ball touches or lies in a hazard you are not allowed to move it or stones or twigs.

If your ball lands in a water hazard you may drop another ball from a specified point but not nearer the hole. A penalty of one shot is added to your score.

Unplayable lie

If your ball lands in such an awkward position that it cannot be played, you are permitted to move the ball according to the rules adding a one stroke penalty to your score. This rule allows you to face your target and, holding your arm in front or to the side, drop the ball two club lengths away from where it lay. This is often safer than attempting to bash the ball out of trouble.

Ground under repair

Ground under repair is an area being repaired by the greenkeeper, usually marked by a small sign. If your ball lands in this area you may lift your ball and drop it without penalty one club length clear of the trouble.

Interference

If your moving ball is stopped or deflected accidentally by another player, it must be played from where it lands. There is no penalty.

The green

Because putting is so important, golfers are allowed to repair pitch marks on the putting surface and clean the ball before putting. Once your ball is on the green you may mark the spot by putting a coin or disk on the ground directly behind the ball and then remove your ball. This is to make sure an opponent's ball does not hit your ball and allows you to clean grass and mud from your ball.

Dropping the ball

The correct way to do this is to extend your arm straight out to the front or to the side, while facing your target, and drop the ball.

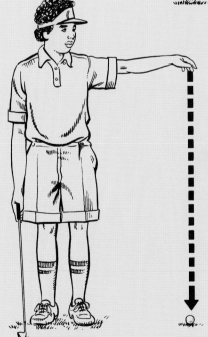

Skills

Grip

The position of your hands on the club will determine how you hit the ball. The object of your grip on the club is to *weld* your hands together so that they work as a unit. How you hold the club has a great bearing on how you will swing the club. The idea is to produce a club swing rather than a body swing. A club swing increases the speed of the club head which makes the ball travel further.

1 Place your left hand under the grip so that the second knuckle of the index finger and the first knuckle of the little finger are aligned under the middle of the grip.

2 Wrap your fingers around the grip without moving the position of your fingers on the grip.

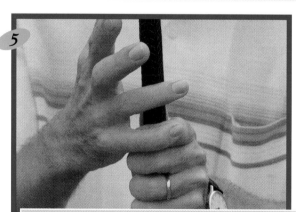

5 Put the little finger of your right hand between your left-hand index and middle finger.

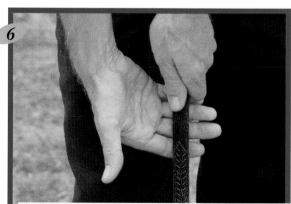

6 The other three fingers of your right hand now wrap around the grip. The first knuckle of the middle finger should be aligned under the middle of the grip.

Overlapping grip

Often called the 'Vardon grip' – after six time British Open winner Harry Vardon – this grip involves the little finger of the right hand sitting between the index and middle fingers of the left hand.

The overlapping grip is the most common and the best suited to beginning players. Take a step-by-step approach to getting the correct grip. The instructions below apply for a right-handed golfer; for a left-handed golfer everything is the same only with the opposite hands.

3

Place the heel of your hand onto the top of the grip.

4

Place your left thumb down so that it sits a little to the right of the centre of the grip. Your thumb and forefinger should now be pushed together.

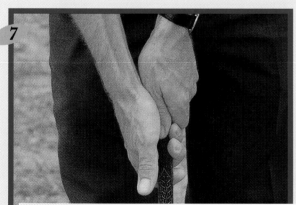

7

Now place the heel of your right thumb on top of your left thumb. Be careful not to push your right hand too far over towards the other hand.

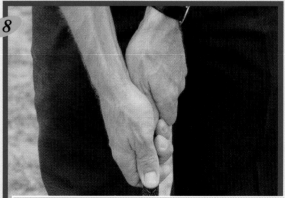

8

Place your right thumb down onto the centre of the grip.

Skills

Address

The address position refers to how you set yourself up to hit the ball.

There are three main aspects to the correct address position:

- alignment
- ball position
- posture.

Alignment

Golf is a game of hitting the ball from where it is sitting to certain targets. To be successful at this you need to be aimed at those targets.

To begin, you must select your target. (It can help if you walk behind your ball so you can see the line between the ball and your target.) Place the club head directly behind the ball so that the club face is aimed at the target.

Position your feet so that the line between your toes is parallel to the imaginary line created from your club face to the target.

Ball position

The clubs are different lengths and, therefore, the ball position needs to be altered accordingly. The starting point is in the centre of your stance.

When using the short irons (6, 7, 8 and 9), the pitching wedge or the sand wedge, the shaft of the club on the ground should be in line with the centre of your stance. The ball is just to the left of the centre line.

You should feel relaxed when addressing the ball. Your weight should be evenly balanced, your knees slightly bent and your head tilted so you are looking down to the ball.

When using the longer irons (5, 4, 3, 2 and 1), you need to move your feet 3 centimetres to the right so that the ball is more to the left of your stance.

When using the fairway woods the ball position is different again. (This applies to any wood you might use when the ball is lying directly on the ground, that is, not on a tee.) Wood numbers 3, 4, 5 and 7 are all used from here. In this instance you should move your feet another 3 centimetres to the right.

Finally, if you move another 3 centimetres to the right you will be in the correct position for the number 1 wood (or driver) when the ball is on the tee.

Posture

For good posture when playing golf you should bend the torso slightly forward from the hips, and bend your knees a little. Your arms should hang near to your body.

The swing

The swing is made up of three main parts:
• backswing
• downswing
• follow through.

Backswing

There are two keys to the backswing. To begin the backswing, turn your shoulders around 90 degrees to the right while swinging the arms up.

Once the shoulder turn is complete, bend (or hinge) your wrists to bring the club back further. Try to hinge from your left wrist, as this will help you to maintain control of your swing.

Downswing

The downswing happens very quickly. The main aim is to swing the club down rather

than the body around. Swinging the body around at this point is a common fault of many golfers.

Follow through

The correct follow through, or finish position, should have the club over your left shoulder with your hands near to your left ear. Your chest should be facing your target. Your right foot should also have turned up onto its toe.

For any shot, the follow through should be longer than the backswing. When the follow through is longer than the backswing it creates more acceleration in the swing, which is vital to hitting an accurate shot.

If your legs are straight and stiff or your hands are too high on the grip it can cause you to stand too close or too far away from the ball. Both of these address positions are incorrect.

Skills

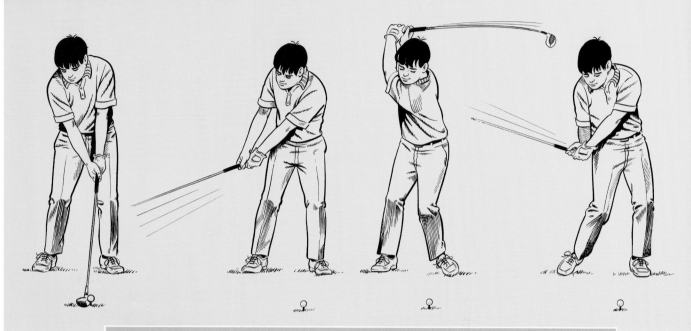

The swing

Swing the club head back slowly and deliberately. Your head must stay completely still and in line with the ball. Move the club back with your hands, arms, hips and shoulders all moving together. Your shoulders should turn from the very beginning of the backswing. Your hips will turn and your weight will be transferred to your back foot (the foot furthest from the hole).

At the top of the backswing your shoulders should have turned approximately 90 degrees and your hips approximately 45 degrees.

During the downswing your hips and shoulders will turn and your weight will start to shift from your back foot to your front foot. Try to hit the ball with the club head travelling parallel to the ground. Even after you have hit the ball your head should still be looking down at the spot where the ball was.

At the finish of the swing the club should have swung right around to rest behind and over your shoulder. Most of your weight will be on your front foot and your chest should face your target.

Skills

The short game

The short game is referred to as such because the clubs used are shorter than the others in the bag and the ball is hit a much shorter distance. The four main areas of the short game are:
- pitching
- chipping
- sand shots
- putting.

Pitching

This is a shot played when you are 15 to 40 metres away from the green. Because of the vast range of distances involved in hitting different **pitch** shots, there are many variations.

Golf course etiquette

When you play golf you are expected to be courteous and to play by the rules. You are also expected to treat other players and the course with respect. All of this is known as golf course etiquette.
- When you want to play a round of golf you will be assigned a tee time. Make sure that you have completed your warm-up and be ready to tee off on time.
- After teeing off, the player whose ball lands furthest from the hole plays first.

Play your shots without delay and then move quickly out of the way.
- If you have lost your ball or if your group is playing noticeably slower than those behind you, let the next group play through rather than holding them up.
- When you hit the fairway and take a **divot** with your swing, stop to replace it. Pick up the divot, replace it in the bare space and step on it to push it back down.
- Sometimes your ball will leave an indentation when it lands on the green. Repair these marks by inserting a pitch repairer

If your ball is about 40 metres from the hole, you would probably take a pitching wedge and swing a little less than a full swing. For young players, a full swing with a pitching wedge might travel about 70–80 metres. Therefore, if you only need to hit the ball 40 metres, you need to use less power. It is vital that you make this deduction in the correct area of the swing – the backswing. To hit shorter shots you need to reduce your amount of backswing.

As you get closer to the green, up to 15 metres away, further reduce the backswing and follow through equally.

Pitching
Pitching is essentially the same as a full swing, only with a shorter backswing. Reducing the backswing reduces the distance the ball will travel. Even as you reduce the backswing for shorter and shorter shots, you should still follow through the same amount.

under the depression. Gently press down so that the tip elevates the turf to the normal level. Repairing all ball marks will ensure that the greens are smoother and easier to putt on for everyone.

• When you hit from a sand bunker, rake the sand smooth as you leave. Rake out all foot and club prints. If there is no rake then use the back of your club.

• When you are on the green and one of your fellow players has a long putt, you should tend the flag. Stand with one hand on the flagstick and remove it as the ball approaches. Handle the flag carefully – being especially careful not to damage the sides of the hole.

• Whilst another player is hitting or putting it is courteous to be quiet and still so they can concentrate. When someone is about to strike a ball be sure that you are not in that player's line of sight. Stay to the side or behind. Never allow your shadow to cross the path of another player's putt.

• The time to fill in your scorecard is while you are waiting to tee off, not while you are still on the green.

Skills

Chipping

This is the shot used when you are less than 15 metres from the green.

The only change to grip and stance for a **chip** shot is that your feet should be closer together. As far as the swing is concerned, it is just shorter than the one used for pitching. When chipping, your wrists should not bend at any time during the swing.

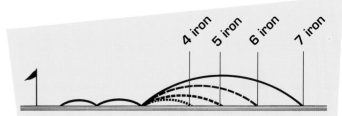

Higher numbered irons will lift the ball higher and further than lower numbered irons. The iron you choose to use will depend on how far you are from the hole and the conditions.

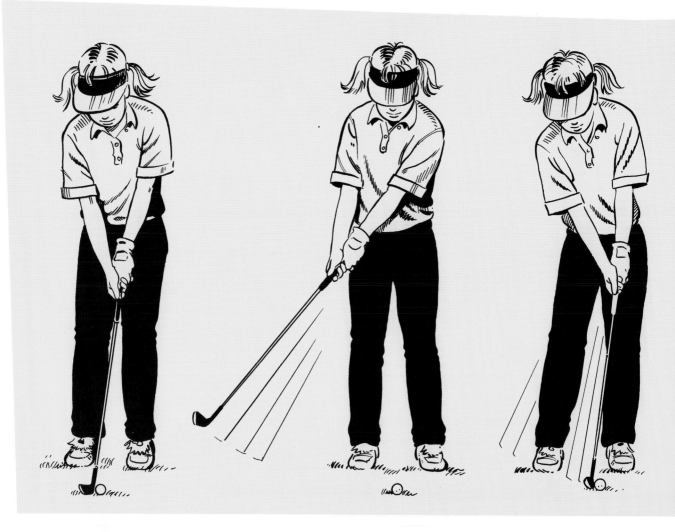

Which club is used for chipping?

This depends on where the hole is in relation to the ball, or whether the ball needs to cross any hazardous conditions, such as a bunker. Imagine that the ball is about 5 metres from the edge of the green:

• if the hole is only 6 metres further on from the edge of the green, you only want the ball to roll a short distance once it lands on the green. The club to use for this shot would be the pitching wedge. The pitching wedge has a lot of angle. This will make the ball fly high into the air and land soft, which produces little run.

• if the hole is 12 metres from the edge of the green, you need the ball to roll more to cover the extra distance. You should take an 8 iron. This club has a straight face which makes the ball fly lower through the air, but roll more when it lands.

• if the hole is 18 metres from the edge of the green, you need an even straighter faced club – a 6 iron. The ball will fly even lower through the air and roll further still when it lands on the green.

For each of these three shots the swing would be exactly the same. Using the different clubs makes the shots different.

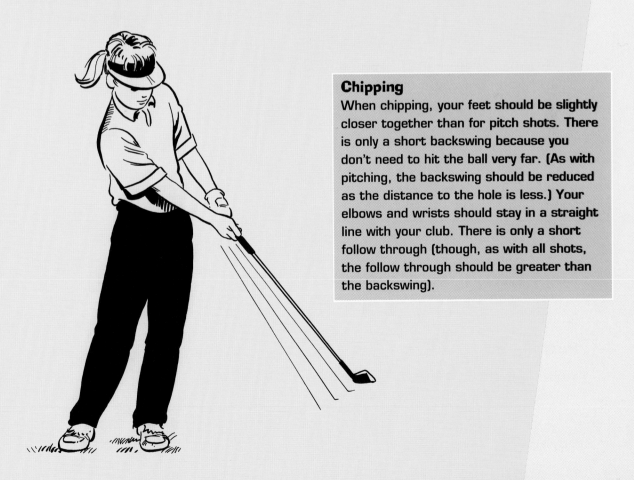

Chipping
When chipping, your feet should be slightly closer together than for pitch shots. There is only a short backswing because you don't need to hit the ball very far. (As with pitching, the backswing should be reduced as the distance to the hole is less.) Your elbows and wrists should stay in a straight line with your club. There is only a short follow through (though, as with all shots, the follow through should be greater than the backswing).

Skills

Sand shot

At many golf courses there are often bunkers around the putting green. In your set of clubs there is a club specifically designed for getting the ball out of the sand. This is the sand iron. The sand iron is usually marked with an 'S', 'SI' or 'SW' on the bottom of the club head.

There are a number of features to successful sand play:

- Make sure you have a firm stance – swivel your shoes into the sand.
- Look at a place in the sand about 2.5 centimetres behind the ball.
- Use the pitching swing or full swing, depending how close the hole is to where you are playing from.
- Hit the sand behind the ball rather than the ball itself (about 2.5 centimetres behind the ball).
- Follow through as you would for the full swing.

To play according to the rules, remember not to touch the sand with your club when setting up for the shot, and always rake the sand smooth when leaving the bunker.

Putting

Once your ball is on the putting green you should use the putter to finish off the hole (to hit the ball into the hole).

There is one important change to the putting grip – to reverse the overlapping fingers. Whereas, previously, the little finger of the right (lower) hand sat over the index finger of the left (higher) hand, when putting the left index finger should sit on top of the right little finger. This helps to keep your wrists locked which is vital for good putting.

The stance for putting is the same as for a short iron stroke. That is, the putter head

Putting
Keep your address still and relaxed. Your eyes should be directly over the ball. Take the putter back low to the ground.

should face the target, your feet should be parallel and the ball position is left of centre. The only change is to position your eyes over the top of the ball.

The putting stroke is essentially the same as chipping. Your wrists should remain locked. The follow through is longer than the backswing – and the further the ball is from the hole, the greater the backswing.

A good reference for the correct amount of backswing required is to swing back 5 centimetres for every metre of distance to the hole. For example, a 4 metre putt would require about 20 centimetres of backswing.

When putting you should change your grip by reversing your overlapping fingers, so that your index finger is on top of your little finger.

Stroke smoothly through the ball. Keep your head down until well after the ball is on its way to the hole.

Skills

Playing a hole

Different players will approach the same hole in different ways. However, how the golfer hits a shot – and where the ball finishes – have the greatest effect on the way a hole is played.

1

Two players are about to play a par 4, 370 metre hole that dog-legs to the left. Maddie, who scored lower than Andrew on the previous hole, has the **honour**. Having checked that players ahead are out of her range, she tees the ball between the ladies' markers and hits her drive into a water hazard 130 metres from the tee.

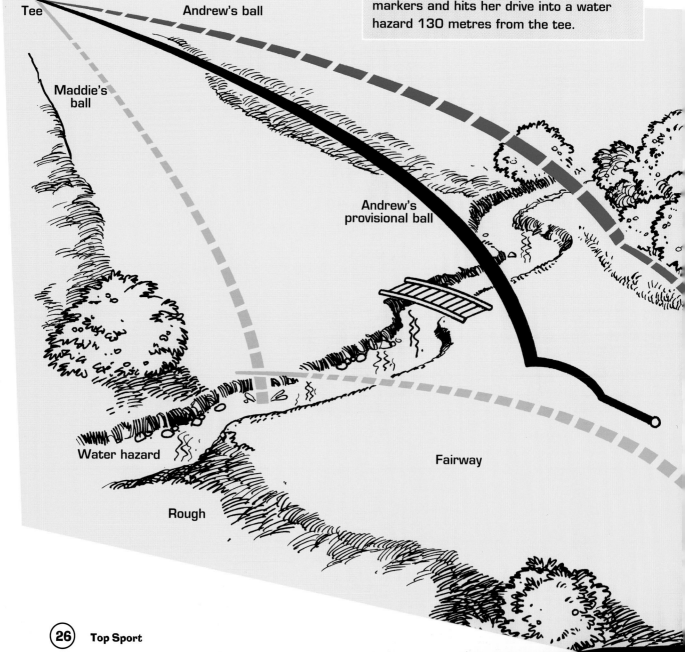

Tee

Andrew's ball

Maddie's ball

Andrew's provisional ball

Water hazard

Fairway

Rough

2

Andrew tees up between the mens' markers and hooks his drive into the rough – apparently out of bounds. He announces that he will hit a **provisional ball** and drives it 210 metres down the fairway.

3

Maddie retrieves her ball from the water hazard, faces the hole and drops the ball. She has had two strokes as she had to add one **penalty shot** for lifting the ball from the stream. With her number 3 wood she hits her next shot 140 metres.

4

Andrew discovers that his ball is not out of bounds so he must play it and retrieve his provisional ball. His drive is in a deep hollow where trees block a clear shot to the green. He chooses a number 7 iron and plays the ball out onto the fairway, just behind Maddie's ball. He uses a number 7 iron for his **approach** shot and hits the ball to the back of the green and onto the apron (the close-mown area around the green).

5

Maddie's ball is about 100 metres from the green. She uses a number 6 iron and hits the ball into a bunker adjacent to the green.

6

Andrew, using a number 5 iron, runs the ball to within two metres of the hole. He then marks it with a disc and removes his ball from the green. This leaves a clear path for Maddie to hit her next shot.

7

Maddie uses her sand wedge in the bunker and hits the ball up onto the green, about three metres from the hole. As she leaves the bunker she rakes the sand behind her. Andrew removes the flagstick for Maddie, who sinks her putt for a double bogie six. She is two shots over par.

8

Andrew replaces his ball on the green and he sinks his putt for a bogie. His score is five – one over par.

Sand trap

Green

Sand trap

9

Maddie returns the flagstick to the cup and immediately walks off the green with Andrew towards the tee. Andrew tallies the score – he will have the honour on the next hole.

Getting ready

It is important to stretch and warm-up before exercising or playing sport. Warming-up will make you more flexible and your muscles and joints will loosen up. This helps you to play your best from the start.

Double hamstring stretch
Sit on the floor with both legs straight out in front of you. While keeping your knees flat on the ground, reach forward with both hands and try to touch your toes. Hold the stretch for 5 seconds. Repeat 6 times, trying to reach further with each stretch.

Shoulder stretch
Hold your elbow and pull your arm across to your chest until you feel the stretch. Hold the stretch for 5 seconds. Repeat on the other side. Repeat 3 times for each shoulder.

Cross-legged, upright hamstring stretch
Stand upright with your legs straight and your right foot crossed over your left foot. With a golf club in both hands, reach down and forward. Hold the stretch for 4 seconds. Now cross your left foot in front of your right foot. Repeat the same stretch. Stretch each way 4 times.

Twist and turn

Stand upright with your feet shoulder-width apart. Hold a golf club horizontally across the back of your shoulders. Twist your body to one side and then the other, trying to twist a little further each time. Repeat 8 times to each side.

Overhead club stretch

Stand upright holding a golf club above your head. While maintaining an upright body position, lean to one side and then to the other. Hold the stretch for 3 seconds on each side. Repeat 6 times to each side.

Seated twist

Hold the club with your hands about one metre apart. Sit on the floor with your left leg bent and crossed over the top of your right leg. Twist your body and stretch to the right. Now bend and cross your right leg over the top of your left leg. Twist your body and stretch to the left. Twist 8 times to each side.

Side bends

Stand upright and place one hand just above your waist. Raise your other arm up and over your head. Bend your body sideways to feel the stretch down one side of your body. Repeat to the other side. Stretch 6 times each side.

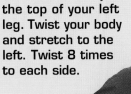

Arm stretch

Lift and bend your arm putting your hands behind your head. Pull the elbow across and back with your other hand.

Taking it further

Many clubs are now encouraging junior members. There are often free golf lessons or introductory courses run during school holidays. Look in your Yellow Pages to get the names and addresses of near-by driving ranges or clubs. Find out if they have any schemes to encourage juniors.

The Sports Council is making grants to the counties to bring more juniors into golf.

Useful names and addresses
The Sports Council
16 Upper Woburn Place
London WC1H 0QP
☎ 0171 273 1500

The Royal and Ancient Golf Club
St Andrews
Fife KY16 9JD
☎ 01344 472112

Note: in the British Isles men's and women's golf is organized separately.

English Golf Union
National Golf Centre
The Broadway
Woodhall Spa
Lincs LN10 6PU
☎ 01526 354500

Scottish Golf Union
Scottish National Golf Centre
Drumoig
Leuchars
Fife KY16 0BE
☎ 01382 549505

Welsh Golf Union
Catsash
Newport
Gwent NP16 1JQ
☎ 01633 430830

Irish Golf Union (for all Ireland)
Glencar House
81 Eglington Road
Donnybrook
Dublin 4
☎ 00353 1269 4111

English Ladies Golf Association
Edgebaston Golf Club
Church Road
Birmingham   B15 3TB
☎ 0121 456 2088

Irish Ladies Golf Association (all Ireland)
1 Clonskeagh Square
Clonskeagh Road
Dublin 14
☎ 00353 1269 6244

Further reading

Nicklaus, J. *Total Golf Techniques*, Treasure Press, London, 1989.
Price, N. *The Ultimate Encyclopedia of Golf*, Carlton Publishing, London, 1995.

Glossary

approach the shots hit to the green.

bunker a hazard filled with sand, occasionally called a sand trap.

chip a short shot to the green.

divot a section of turf uplifted when hitting a ball.

fairway the area of the course between the teeing ground and the green.

flagstick a pole with a small flag at the top that is placed in the hole to provide a target for the player; also called the pin.

green the putting surface of the course.

handicap a figure to indicate the average difference between a golfer's score and the par of the course.

hazard a bunker, pond, stream or ditch.

hole the target on the green, also the complete area from tee to hole.

honour commencing the play on a particular hole, given to the player who records the lowest score on the previous hole.

iron a club with a thin metal head and a shorter shaft than a wood.

out of bounds when the ball is hit over the boundary of the course.

par the score allocated to a hole or a course according to its level of difficulty.

penalty shot a stroke (or strokes) added to a player's score because of a breach of the rules.

pitch a high lofted shot played from near the green.

provisional ball when a ball is thought to be lost or out of bounds (except for a water hazard) to save time a player may play another ball from as near as possible to where the original ball was played before walking forward.

putt the stroke played with a putter on the greens.

putter a metal club used on the short grass of the putting green.

sand shot a shot hit when the ball is in a sand bunker.

stroke the striking or hitting of the ball.

tee the wooden or plastic peg on which the ball is placed before driving off, also used to refer to the area from which the tee shot is played.

tee shot the first shot at each hole.

water hazard a pond or stream over which the ball must travel.

wedge a type of club used to hit the ball up into the air.

wood a club with a longer shaft than an iron, traditionally with a wooden head but now often made of metal, used to hit the ball long distances.

Index